Original title:
The Warmth of Winter Evenings

Copyright © 2024 Creative Arts Management OÜ
All rights reserved.

Author: Ethan Prescott
ISBN HARDBACK: 978-9916-94-446-2
ISBN PAPERBACK: 978-9916-94-447-9

Whispered Fireside Tales

Around the fire, shadows dance,
Stories weave in a gentle trance.
Voices low, with laughter shared,
Every heart knows they're cared.

A Blanket of Stars

In the night, the heavens gleam,
Wishes float like a silent dream.
Each star tells of forgotten days,
While moonlight wraps in silver rays.

Hushed Footprints in the Snow

Crisp and white, the ground lies still,
Footprints mark where hearts will thrill.
Every step a silent song,
In the hush, we all belong.

Glow of Dusk

As day fades into evening's hue,
The sky blushes with colors true.
Whispers of night begin to rise,
In the glow, our spirits fly.

Ribbons of Smoke

In the quiet night sky, they dance,
Delicate tendrils, lost in a trance.
Whispers of stories, wreathed in grey,
Carried on breezes, floating away.

Curling and twisting, soft as a sigh,
Memories linger, then fade and die.
Echoes of laughter, shadows of light,
Ribbons of smoke in the pale moonlight.

Gathering by the Glow

In the hearth's warm embrace, we convene,
Flickering shadows dance, lively and keen.
Stories are woven, laughter takes flight,
Gathering by the glow, hearts feel so right.

The fire crackles, sparks leap and curl,
Revealing soft secrets, each flicker a pearl.
Voices entwined, a tapestry spun,
Gathering by the glow, two become one.

Frosty Breath and Flickering Flames

In the chill of the night, breaths turn to mist,
Frosty whispers embrace those we've kissed.
Flames leap and shimmer, a bright, warm dance,
Warding away shadows, igniting romance.

Crackling wood sings a song of delight,
Flickering flames chase away the cold night.
In this cozy circle, we savor the heat,
Frosty breath mingles, heartbeats in sync.

Solace in Solitude

In the silence of night, a stillness unfolds,
Whispers of nature, secrets untold.
Moments of peace, cradled in thought,
Finding the solace that solitude brought.

Beneath the vast sky, stars quietly gleam,
Lost in reflection, embracing the dream.
Here in the quiet, I am truly free,
Solace in solitude, just the stars and me.

Hearthside Reflections

By the fire's glow, shadows dance,
Whispers of warmth, a subtle trance.
Memories flicker, tales unfold,
As embers burn bright, and stories are told.

The crackle sings a soothing tune,
While outside, the chill of a silver moon.
Faces aglow, love softly shared,
In this sacred space, we are unpaired.

Icicles and Candlelight

Icicles dangle like crystal tears,
Holding the whispers of winter's years.
Candlelight flickers, a warm embrace,
Chasing the chill from night's cold face.

Outside the world is frosted and still,
While inside hearts glow, a cozy thrill.
Shadows play on the walls so pale,
As stories of old on the night winds sail.

Midnight's Soft Serenade

The clock strikes twelve, a hush in the air,
As dreams take flight, free from despair.
Moonlight spills through a silken pane,
A serenade whispers, sweet and plain.

Stars twinkle gently, a lullaby's grace,
In the quiet night, we find our place.
Reflection dances on the silver sea,
In midnight's arms, we are truly free.

Chasing Shadows in the Cold

Frosted breath mingles, the dark takes hold,
As we chase shadows out in the cold.
Footsteps crunch softly on paths unknown,
In winter's embrace, together we've grown.

With laughter and warmth, we roam the night,
In search of stars and winter's light.
The chill may bite, but hearts stay warm,
In a world of shadows, we find our charm.

Cradled in Winter's Serenade

Snowflakes whisper on the breeze,
A hush that falls and gently frees.
The world adorned in softest white,
A tranquil quilt, a starry night.

Branches bow with a frosty sigh,
While shadows dance as day goes by.
In this stillness, dreams take flight,
Cradled warm in winter's light.

Embers in the Twilight

As daylight fades to shades of gray,
Embers glow, a warm bouquet.
The sky ignites in fiery hues,
A canvas brushed with evening's muse.

Whispers carry through the air,
Secrets shared, a gentle dare.
Together, hearts intertwine,
Embers spark, our souls align.

Frost-Kissed Embrace

A frosty breath upon my skin,
Nature's kiss, where love begins.
The world around us sparkles bright,
In frosted dreams, we hold on tight.

Each step crunches underfoot,
In this moment, our hearts commute.
With laughter shared in the chill,
A warm embrace that time can't still.

Lanterns in the Snow

Lanterns glow with golden light,
Guiding wanderers through the night.
In snowflakes swirling, stories told,
Of dreams ignited, brave and bold.

Beneath the stars, each path we trace,
Hope reflected in every face.
Together we find our way to go,
Illuminated by lanterns in the snow.

Tender Flames and Winter's Embrace

Tender flames flicker bright,
Dancing in the night's cool air.
Winter's breath, a gentle bite,
Wrapped in warmth, without a care.

Snowflakes swirl, a silent song,
In this moment, time will freeze.
Holding close where we belong,
Hearts entwined with perfect ease.

Twilight's Embrace on Chilled Cheeks

Twilight whispers soft and low,
Chilled cheeks kissed by fading light.
Stars begin their evening show,
As shadows dance, the world feels right.

A cozy nook, a gentle glow,
Under blankets, laughter flows.
In this moment, love will grow,
While the brisk night air bestows.

Stars Above, Warmth Below

Stars above, they gleam and shine,
A tapestry of dreams untold.
Warmth below, two hearts entwined,
In each other's arms, we hold.

Nature's canvas, vast and wide,
In the stillness, feelings blend.
With every sigh, the stars confide,
In this love that knows no end.

Sipping Joy from a Mug

Sipping joy from a cozy mug,
Steam rises, filling the air.
Each warm sip, a gentle hug,
Whispers of comfort everywhere.

Outside, the world is chilly,
But here, a fire crackles bright.
Wrapped in laughter, oh so silly,
Every moment feels just right.

Icicles and Intimacy

Hanging from eaves, they glisten bright,
Cold treasures formed, in the pale moonlight.
Whispers of winter, we draw so near,
In frozen moments, our warmth is clear.

Together we breathe, steam in the air,
Fingers entwined, without a care.
Icicles quiver, against the window's pane,
Our hearts beat softly, a sweet refrain.

Hearts Wrapped in Wool

In cozy corners, where shadows hide,
Woolen threads twine, with love as our guide.
Sip steaming cider, share laughter and cheer,
Wrapped in our blankets, the world disappears.

Fires crackle gently, a warm embrace,
In every heartbeat, we find our place.
Through chilly nights, the winds may howl,
But in this haven, we softly prowl.

Chasing Shadows of Frost

Under the moon, we tread with grace,
Chasing shadows, in a frozen place.
Each step a whisper, the world is still,
Frosted dreams, our hearts can fill.

A dance with the night, where spirits soar,
Crisp air beckons, inviting us more.
We trace the patterns that nature draws,
In the chill of winter, we find our cause.

Lullabies of the Winter Night

Softly it falls, the snowflakes' dance,
In silence they sing, a tranquil romance.
Lullabies echo, beneath the stars,
A gentle embrace, erasing our scars.

Wrapped in the night, dreams take their flight,
Each breath a promise, a warm, soft light.
The world outside sleeps, in blankets so deep,
While lullabies soothe, our hearts softly leap.

A Gentle Hearth

The flames flicker soft and bright,
Casting shadows in the night.
A warmth that wraps around the room,
Bringing solace, chasing gloom.

In the corner, a chair does wait,
Inviting dreams, whispering fate.
Stories shared and laughter spilled,
In this space, our hearts are filled.

A crackling sound, a soothing hum,
In this haven, worries succumb.
The hearth's embrace, a loving touch,
Here we gather, oh so much.

With every ember, with every spark,
We find our peace, within the dark.
A gentle hearth, where love is found,
In this warmth, our souls abound.

Dreams in the Embers

In the glow of fading light,
Whispers dance, taking flight.
Embers glow with secrets shared,
Dreams unfold, tenderly bared.

The night is quiet, the world slows,
In the warmth, our spirit grows.
Floating wishes on the breeze,
Carried softly, hearts at ease.

Each spark a promise in the air,
Flickering hope, a gentle prayer.
In this moment, time feels right,
Lost in dreams, beneath the night.

Together we weave stories bright,
In the cool embrace of night.
What's kindled here, may never fade,
In the embers, dreams are made.

Moonlit Fireside Reverie

By the fire's flickering glow,
Moonlight dances, soft and slow.
Whispers float upon the breeze,
Tales of love bring us to ease.

Silver beams on faces bright,
Ellis entwined in the night.
Each glance shared, a story spun,
In this magic, we are one.

Crackling laughs, the night unfolds,
Secrets shared and truths retold.
In the moon's embrace, we dream,
Fireside warmth, a gentle beam.

Every shadow sings of peace,
In this moment, worries cease.
Moonlit fires, a sacred space,
In this glow, we find our grace.

A Cup of Comfort

Steam rising from the gentle mug,
In its warmth, a sweet snug hug.
Sipping slowly, feeling whole,
Each taste a balm for the soul.

Moments linger, time stands still,
In our hearts, we feel the thrill.
A cup of comfort, shared with friends,
Creating joy that never ends.

As laughter dances, spirits rise,
In every smile, a sweet surprise.
Tea or coffee, it matters not,
In this space, we share our thoughts.

With every sip, we find our place,
In the warmth of love's embrace.
A cup of comfort, pure and bright,
Filling our hearts with pure delight.

Embers Whispering Glow

In the hearth, the embers sway,
Softly dancing, night to day.
Whispers linger, stories told,
In the warmth, we find our gold.

Flickering light, shadows play,
Hearts are warmed, as we stay.
Secrets shared in the fire's embrace,
Time stands still, a sacred space.

Breath of winter, crisp and clear,
In the glow, no room for fear.
Each spark that rises, dreams ignite,
Together here, the world feels right.

Frost-Kissed Fireside Dreams

Outside the chill, a world of white,
Inside, the fire casts its light.
Blankets wrapped, we close our eyes,
In this moment, love flies high.

Frosty windows, patterns seen,
A canvas kissed by winter's sheen.
Each crackle brings a gentle sigh,
In dreams, we soar, together high.

Hot cocoa steams, a sweet delight,
Fireside whispers, hearts so light.
As stars sparkle in the night sky,
We hold this magic, you and I.

Solace in Candlelight

Candle flames flicker, shadows dance,
In their glow, we take a chance.
Softly spoken words of peace,
Heavy hearts find sweet release.

The fragrance of wax and smoke,
In silence, tender bonds we stoke.
Each candle lit, a wish unfurls,
Creating warmth that gently whirls.

In candlelight, our worries fade,
Cocooned in love, we are remade.
Time slips away like grains of sand,
Together here, hand in hand.

Cozy Conversations

In the corner, laughter rings,
Stories shared, as comfort clings.
Tea and warmth blend in the air,
In cozy nooks, we have no care.

Words like fire, glowing bright,
Illuminating the quiet night.
Each voice a melody, soft and clear,
Building bonds that draw us near.

Familiar tales and dreams anew,
With every sip, our spirits grew.
Wrapped in friendship, time will pause,
In these moments, love finds cause.

Sips of Comfort

In the mug, warmth swirls,
A dance of steam and spice,
Each sip a gentle hug,
A moment soft and nice.

The world fades far away,
Wrapped in cozy embrace,
With every drop, I stay,
In this serene space.

Chocolate drips so sweet,
Sugar kisses the soul,
In each warm heartbeat,
I find my quiet whole.

As night drapes its cloak,
I cradle my delight,
In this gentle soak,
Sips of joy ignite.

The Stillness of Warmth

Candles flicker low,
Casting shadows that sway,
Whispers in the glow,
As night slips softly away.

Wrapped in woolen threads,
Outside, the chill bites deep,
Yet here, hope treads,
In warmth, we breathe, weleep.

The clock ticks slowly on,
Time softens, feels divine,
Moments stretch and yawn,
In this quiet, we shine.

Embers gently burn,
As stories fill the air,
In stillness, we learn,
Together, we share.

Puzzles in the Frost

Beneath a sky of gray,
Frost weaves its icy lace,
Each pattern a ballet,
Nature's tender embrace.

Crystals on windowpanes,
Secrets held in their gleam,
Here, beauty remains,
In the chill, we dream.

Glimmers of silver light,
A world transformed anew,
With each breath, so bright,
I witness magic, true.

As morning dew will fade,
The puzzles melt away,
In memory, they're laid,
A fleeting, cold ballet.

Songs of a Quiet Night

The stars hum soft and low,
A lullaby of light,
Casting dreams that flow,
Through the stillness of night.

Crickets play their tune,
Waves of whispers sway,
While the silver moon,
Keeps the dark at bay.

Each note a gentle kiss,
Spinning tales of old,
In this sweet abyss,
Their melodies unfold.

As slumber draws near,
Wrapped in night's embrace,
The songs, crystal clear,
Guide my heart's slow pace.

Raindrops Turning to Snow

Raindrops fall, a gentle sound,
Whispers in the air abound.
Gray clouds weave a winter tale,
As icy breezes start to wail.

Frosty flakes begin to dance,
Twinkling in a fleeting chance.
They blanket earth in purest white,
Turning day into cozy night.

Laughter echoes, children play,
In this magic, winter's sway.
Raindrops shift to snowy bliss,
A fleeting touch we can't dismiss.

Underneath the twilight's glow,
Nature's wonders start to show.
A world transformed, all aglow,
Raindrops turning to soft snow.

Beneath Cozy Blankets

Fires crackle, shadows dance,
In this moment, I find chance.
Beneath blankets, snug and tight,
Wrapped in warmth, I greet the night.

Pages turn, a story unfolds,
Whispers of adventures bold.
With every word, my heart ignites,
Comfort lives in gentle sights.

Outside, winter winds may roar,
But here inside, I want no more.
Cocoa warms my smiling face,
In this cherished, cozy space.

Dreams take flight with every sigh,
As stars twinkle in the sky.
Beneath blankets, love does grow,
In this haven, safe from snow.

Sugar and Spice Stories

Once upon a time in a land,
Where sugar spun like golden sand.
Spice danced in the warm air,
Stories waiting, none to spare.

There were fairies, bright and small,
With laughter echoing through the hall.
Gingerbread houses, candy trees,
A world created just to please.

Magic flowed in every bite,
As day transformed to magical night.
In every tale, a lesson shines,
Love and friendship intertwines.

Sugar and spice, they told their tale,
With whispers sweet that never pale.
In dreams and stories, hearts entwined,
In this wonder, joy we'll find.

Soft Glows and Cool Nights

Soft glows flicker, candles sway,
On this calm, enchanting day.
Cool nights cradle dreams so deep,
Whispers from the stars we keep.

Moonlight weaves through branches bare,
Casting shadows, oh so rare.
In the hush, our secrets sigh,
As fireflies dance, drifting high.

Warmth of friendship fills the air,
In this moment, free from care.
Laughter mingles, hearts collide,
In soft glows, we find our guide.

Cool nights bring our spirits near,
Wrapped in love, we have no fear.
Together under twilight skies,
We cherish life, where beauty lies.

A Blanket of Stillness

In the hush of the night, a soft sigh,
Winter's breath lingers, as shadows fly.
Each flake a whisper, dance in the air,
Nature's embrace, a moment to share.

Trees wear their gowns of shimmering white,
Cradled in silence, lost from the light.
A quilted horizon, where dreams take flight,
A blanket of stillness, wrapping the night.

Moonlight Drapes the Snow

Gentle beams weave through the darkened trees,
Moonlight drapes the snow, its softest freeze.
A silver glow bathes the world in peace,
As shadowed corners find their sweet release.

Footsteps crackle through the deep drifts,
Every step forward, a mystery lifts.
In this quiet realm, where magic flows,
Beneath the blanket, the stillness grows.

Hearthside Reflections

By the fire's light, stories unfold,
Warmth of the hearth against the cold.
Faces aglow, laughter in the air,
Time lingers here, a bond we all share.

Memories dance in the flickering flames,
Echoes of voices, familiar names.
Each crackle a tale, spun through the years,
In hearthside reflections, joy disappears.

Whispered Secrets Beneath the Stars

Under a canopy, vast and bright,
Whispered secrets float into the night.
Constellations listen, ancient and wise,
As dreams intertwine with the starlit skies.

The cool breeze carries soft, tender sighs,
Moments shared under the watchful eyes.
A tapestry woven of wishes and fears,
Beneath the stars' glow, the world disappears.

When the World Sleeps Beneath White

Snow blankets the soft ground,
Whispers of silence abound.
Trees wear coats of icy lace,
Under stars, the world finds grace.

Hushed are the bustling streets,
Footsteps fade, a calm retreat.
Moonlight dances on the snow,
In the stillness, hearts aglow.

Children dream of winter's play,
While the night gently sways.
Frozen breath, a fleeting sight,
When the world sleeps, all feels right.

As dawn hints with rosy hue,
Nature stirs, a scene so new.
Beneath white, the world awakes,
In the silence, joy it makes.

Echoes of Laughter in Chill

Beneath the pale winter sun,
Laughter dances, warmth begun.
Frosty air, but spirits gleam,
Friendship flows like a flowing stream.

Chill bites at our rosy cheeks,
Yet the joy each moment speaks.
With every grin and playful tease,
We find comfort, hearts at ease.

Snowflakes fall and twirl around,
Life's soft melody, a sweet sound.
Echoes fill the crisp, cold air,
In laughter, we are free from care.

A tapestry of memory spun,
In each moment, we have won.
Hearts entwined through cold and thrill,
Together, laughter warms the chill.

Trails of Smoke in the Evening Sky

As twilight falls, a fire glows,
Smoke trails up where the night rose.
Stars peek through the darkened veil,
In the distance, whispers sail.

Each breath rises, a soft sigh,
Stories linger in the sky.
Embers dance, a fleeting spark,
Guiding dreams into the dark.

Time slows down, the world serene,
In the warmth, a tranquil scene.
Nature listens, all is still,
In the night, we find our will.

Connected by the evening air,
Every glance, a silent prayer.
Trails of smoke, our hopes set free,
In the twilight, just you and me.

Comfort Found in Shared Glances

In crowded rooms, our eyes collide,
A silent language, hearts confide.
With just a look, the world is still,
In that moment, we feel the thrill.

Worries fade, time drifts away,
In shared glances, we find our way.
Understanding flows without a sound,
In our gazes, solace is found.

Through laughter bright and shadows cast,
In fleeting glances, moments last.
Each gaze a thread, woven tight,
Creating warmth in the soft light.

Together, we conquer distant fears,
In every look, we've shared the years.
Comfort blooms, in silence dance,
In shared glances, love's own chance.

Pine Scented Whispers

In the forest deep and green,
Whispers linger, soft and keen.
Pine scents dance upon the air,
Nature's secrets, rich and rare.

Underneath the towering trees,
Gentle rustling in the breeze.
Echoes of a tranquil sound,
Harmony where peace is found.

Sunlight filters through the pine,
Casting shadows, light divine.
A haven for the heart and soul,
In the woods, we feel whole.

Pine scented whispers call to me,
A symphony, wild and free.
Holding tight to nature's grace,
In these woods, we find our place.

Peppermint and Pleasure

Sweet notes from a candy cane,
Minty freshness, sweet refrain.
Dancing on the tongue so bright,
A burst of joy, pure delight.

In the cup of winter's cheer,
Peppermint warms, drawing near.
Lingering laughter fills the air,
Moments shared, love laid bare.

Crushed candies, colors bold,
Memories wrapped, stories told.
With every sip, joy's embrace,
A world of wonder that we trace.

Peppermint dreams on frosty nights,
Softly glowing, warm, and bright.
In this bliss, we take our measure,
Savoring each drop of pleasure.

The Warmth We Share

By the fire's flickering light,
Our hearts twine, holding tight.
Stories spin like glowing flames,
In this space, nothing's the same.

Laughter dances on the air,
Wrapped in love, free from care.
Hand in hand, we find our way,
In each moment, joy alway.

The warmth of souls in gentle grace,
Time slows down, a sacred place.
Eyes that sparkle, love so true,
In our hearts, we feel anew.

Together here, we stand as one,
Under the moon, beneath the sun.
With every heartbeat, we declare,
Life's a treasure that we share.

Nestled in November's Embrace

Golden leaves crunch underfoot,
Crisp air whispers, seasons moot.
Nestled in this twilight glow,
November's warmth begins to show.

Sweaters wrapped, hands interlaced,
In this moment, time's embraced.
Fires crackle, shadows play,
Memories made in soft array.

Pumpkin spice and candlelight,
Autumn's magic, pure delight.
Gathered close, hearts intertwine,
In this haven, all feels fine.

November's chill can't bring us down,
With you here, I wear the crown.
Together through the cool night's grace,
Forever wrapped in love's embrace.

Dreamscapes in the Cold

Underneath a moonlit sky,
Whispers dance in winter's sigh.
Silent dreams of ice and snow,
Guided by the winds that blow.

Shadows cast of silver sheen,
In the night, a world so serene.
Frozen lakes with secrets told,
Wrapped in layers of the cold.

Stars will twinkle, faint and bright,
As we drift into the night.
Chasing visions, soft and bright,
In dreamscapes of the cold's delight.

Vintage Sweaters and Hot Cocoa

Faded colors, woven tight,
Snug against the cold of night.
Patchwork memories to embrace,
Warmth that time cannot erase.

Marshmallows float in mugs of cheer,
Each sip whispers, 'Winter's here.'
Cinnamon dusted on top,
With each warm taste, we won't stop.

Laughter echoes in the air,
As friends gather, warmth to share.
Cozy evenings by the fire,
Hearts ignited, dreams inspire.

Reflections in Frost

Windows etched with icy lace,
Nature's art in every place.
In the morning, sunlight gleams,
Casting light on frozen dreams.

Patterns shift as shadows play,
Morning coffee warms the day.
Every drop, a spark divine,
Reflections meet the frosty line.

Whispers of the winter's breath,
Life and beauty, even in death.
Moments caught in crystal form,
A reminder of winter's charm.

Traditions of Warmth

Candles flicker, soft and bright,
Gathered close on winter nights.
Stories shared, laughter flows,
In our hearts, the fire glows.

Family recipes, passed down too,
Each dish tells of love so true.
Fireside chats and the tales we weave,
In these moments, we believe.

Through the years, the seasons change,
But traditions never rearrange.
The warmth we hold, it lights the way,
Through every night, to greet the day.

Flickering Spirits of the Cold

In winter's grasp, the shadows dance,
Whispers of snow in a fleeting trance.
Chilled breezes carry tales untold,
Flickering spirits, brave and bold.

Beneath the moon's soft silver glow,
Silent secrets in the midnight snow.
A flicker, a spark, then fades away,
Echoes of night where the cold ones play.

Branches groan with a frosty weight,
Entwined with dreams, they navigate.
The warmth of fire, a distant call,
In the heart of winter, we rise and fall.

With each snowflake, a story we weave,
In the cold's embrace, it's hard to believe.
Yet spirits linger, gentle and bright,
Flickering softly through the cold of night.

Embracing the Silence of Snow

The world wraps close in a sheet of white,
A quiet blanket, pure and bright.
Each flake that falls, a whisper soft,
Embracing silence, the heart lifts aloft.

In stillness, thoughts begin to flow,
Captured in moments, the essence of snow.
The breath of winter hangs in the air,
A tranquil space, devoid of care.

Frost-kissed branches sway and sigh,
Glistening under the pale blue sky.
Nature seems to pause and reflect,
In the quietude, time feels perfect.

Each step resounds in the crunching frost,
Together we wander, never lost.
Under the spell of the snowy glow,
We find our peace in the dance of snow.

Stories Spun by the Fire

Around the flame, we gather near,
With crackling logs, the night feels clear.
Tales unfold in the flickering light,
Stories spun, warm hearts ignite.

The embers burn with a soft embrace,
Each word a thread, each laugh a trace.
Memories woven in the amber hue,
In this circle, old feels new.

Ghosts of the past dance in the glow,
With each tale shared, our spirits grow.
Time stands still as the fire sings,
Rekindling joy that friendship brings.

As shadows play on the wooden wall,
We share our dreams, and we share our falls.
The warmth of the fire, the bond we hold,
In our stories spun, we are never old.

Soft Light and Frosty Air

In the dawn, where shadows retreat,
Soft light kisses the frosty street.
The world awakens, all aglow,
In the crisp embrace of winter's show.

Breath like steam in the chilly morn,
Nature's beauty, fresh and reborn.
Each frost-tipped blade, a gem of white,
Whispers of magic in soft daylight.

Birds take flight through the gentle haze,
Songs of the season, winter's praise.
The air is sharp, yet dreams do soar,
In this gentle stillness, we long for more.

With every step on the sparkling floor,
Joy dances close, forever in store.
Soft light and frost, a perfect pair,
In the heart of winter, love fills the air.

Embracing Chills

Winter whispers soft and low,
Frosty breath in evening glow.
Nature's blanket, crisp and white,
Stars will dance in silent night.

Beneath the moon, the world does freeze,
Branches sway in gentle breeze.
Breath of cold paints cheeks with red,
Cozy thoughts of warmth ahead.

Comfort in a Crunch

When worries loom and shadows creep,
Find solace where the heart can leap.
Crunch of leaves beneath the feet,
A moment found, a life complete.

Sipping tea by candlelight,
Whispers heard, hearts feel light.
Laughter shared, a gentle touch,
In the chaos, love does clutch.

Nightfall's Glow

As daylight fades, the stars appear,
Whispers of dusk for all to hear.
Moonlit paths weave through the trees,
A tranquil mind, a soft, cool breeze.

In the quiet, dreams take flight,
Shadows dance in the silver light.
Night's embrace wraps hearts so tight,
In the dark, we find our sight.

Dreaming by the Fire

Crackling flames in the hearth's warm glow,
Stories whispered, tales we know.
As logs pop, embers rise high,
In this moment, time slips by.

Warmth surrounds, and eyes grow dim,
Thoughts take root on a fiery whim.
Nestled close, we share a sigh,
Dreaming softly, just you and I.

Lanterns Against the Dark

In the midnight's soft embrace,
Shadows dance, they lose their place.
With every flicker, hope ignites,
Lanterns glimmer, banishing nights.

Beneath the stars, a guiding flame,
Whispers secrets, calls our name.
Through the silence, light remains,
In every heart, love's gentle chains.

Breaths Visible

In the crisp air, we take a breath,
Exhaling warmth, defying death.
Each fleeting mist a silent plea,
Carried on winds, wild and free.

Moments linger, captured tight,
In the day's glow or the moon's light.
Visible dreams in the chill we face,
Life's essence shared, a warm embrace.

Hearts Open

With every smile, a door ajar,
Inviting light from near and far.
Hearts entwined, we share our fate,
In love's embrace, we celebrate.

The gentle touch of honesty,
Breaking barriers, setting free.
In trust we find our strength revealed,
A tapestry of love, unsealed.

Finding Light in Long Nights

When stars fade and shadows creep,
In the stillness, secrets keep.
Hope arises, softly glows,
A flicker born where darkness grows.

With whispered dreams, we forge our way,
Through winding paths, come what may.
Light emerges, a steadfast guide,
In long nights, hope won't subside.

Moments of Stillness

In the hush of dawn's first light,
Peace descends, banishing night.
Each heartbeat echoes, calm and clear,
In moments cherished, we draw near.

Time suspends in gentle sway,
Inviting thoughts to softly play.
In stillness found, we rest our minds,
Connecting threads that love entwines.

Letters to the Stars

Under the night sky's embrace,
Whispers of dreams take flight.
Ink spills on paper's face,
Wishing upon stars so bright.

Each letter, a piece of my soul,
Carried on the winds of time.
The cosmos keeps my secrets whole,
In constellations, they chime.

Silent echoes of hope and despair,
Woven in the celestial threads.
The universe listens, ever fair,
To musings of hearts and their dreads.

A tapestry of wishes and sighs,
Floating in the cosmic sea.
These letters, like shooting stars, rise,
Connecting you and me.

Tales Wrapped in Wool

In a corner, warm and snug,
Stories whispered, softly spun.
Wrapped in wool, a cozy hug,
As evening's shadows gently run.

Tales of old and futures bright,
Knitted with love and soft delight.
A tapestry of memories tight,
Each thread a moment, pure and right.

Laughter echoes, as yarn unwinds,
Characters come alive and dance.
In every loop, adventure finds,
The heart's soft, enchanted trance.

So gather 'round, let spirits soar,
With every stitch, a world unfolds.
In woolen tales of yore and more,
A treasure chest of stories told.

Muffled Laughter in the Chill

Winter's breath upon the air,
Whispers of joy, soft and light.
Muffled tones of laughter shared,
In the blankets, warm and bright.

Footprints in the snowy white,
Dancing shadows, fleeting time.
In frozen scenes, hearts take flight,
Chasing echoes, spirits climb.

The world draped in a silver sheen,
Each chuckle paints a memory.
In chilly nights, we're serene,
Mirth ignites like a melody.

Cocoa cups, warmth in our palms,
Stories spun 'neath twinkling stars.
In winter's hush, the heart calms,
Laughter lingers, healing scars.

Scent of Pine and Spice

In the air, a fragrant blend,
Pine trees whisper sweet and low.
With each breath, the senses mend,
As autumn's colors start to glow.

Spices dance on the gentle breeze,
Cinnamon hugs the fading light.
Nature's symphony aims to please,
A warm embrace against the night.

Beneath the boughs, stories unfold,
Secrets shared with every sway.
In nature's arms, we feel bold,
Lost in dreams where we can play.

So let the scent guide your way,
Through forest trails and winding streams.
With pine and spice, come what may,
We'll find our joy in fragrant dreams.

Open Hearts in Closed Spaces

In rooms where shadows softly play,
We find the light in what we say.
A whisper shared, a knowing glance,
Our hearts expand, begin to dance.

In silence thick, our dreams take flight,
Together we forge the darkest night.
These walls can't hold our spirits tight,
For love can break through any fright.

With open hearts, we break the mold,
The warmth within, a fire's hold.
In closed spaces, we bloom anew,
With every breath, our hopes accrue.

The world outside may close its door,
Yet inside here, we yearn for more.
In vastness, find what we embrace,
In closed spaces, we find our place.

Respite from the Chill

The frost creeps in, the winds do bite,
Yet in our hearts, a glow ignites.
A fire crackles, warmth profound,
Where laughter's echo can be found.

Beneath the eaves, we find our seat,
With blankets piled at our feet.
Hot cocoa warms our weary souls,
A cherished moment, time extols.

We tell our stories, tales untold,
In winter's clutch, we are consoled.
Outside, the world may freeze and fall,
But here, together, we have it all.

Respite from chill, a haven sweet,
In each other's arms, we find our beat.
Through winter's grasp, we dare to dream,
In cozy nooks, we share the gleam.

A Tapestry of Togetherness

Threads of laughter woven tight,
Colors blending, pure delight.
Each moment shared, a vibrant hue,
A tapestry of me and you.

In patterns rich, we stitch our days,
In every glance, a warm gaze.
Together we face both joy and strife,
Weaving the fabric of our life.

The needle pulls, we gather near,
Sewing our hopes, dispelling fear.
With each embrace, our hearts align,
A tapestry, divine, entwined.

Through storms that come and bonds that fray,
In unity, we find our way.
A work of art, forever blessed,
A tapestry where love's confessed.

Twilight's Caress

As day retreats, the colors blend,
Twilight whispers, start to mend.
A gentle hush descends with grace,
In evening's glow, we find our space.

The sky ablaze with hues serene,
A canvas painted, soft and keen.
In twilight's arms, the world feels right,
A tranquil pause before the night.

Gone are the rush and harsh demands,
With twilight's touch, our hearts make plans.
We breathe in deep the moment's song,
In shadows deep, we all belong.

As stars emerge, they softly gleam,
Within their light, we dare to dream.
In twilight's caress, dreams take flight,
A bridge between the day and night.

Lullabies of Winter

Soft whispers of snow fall,
Blanketing the world in white.
The stars beginning to call,
Embracing the quiet night.

Children's laughter echoes near,
As frost dances on the glass.
Hearts warmed by love held dear,
In moments that softly pass.

Cold winds sing their gentle song,
Through trees that sway and bend.
In the silence, we belong,
As winter nights gently blend.

Hot cocoa warms chilly hands,
While stories unfold with grace.
In this land of snowy strands,
We find peace in this embrace.

Hearthstone Memories

Crackling flames in the night,
Casting shadows on the wall.
Whispers shared by firelight,
Where stories rise and softly fall.

Worn armchairs hold our dreams,
As embers glow with tender heat.
Every laugh, a golden beam,
In memories cozy and sweet.

Tales of love and journeys made,
Echo softly in the air.
In fireside warmth, we wade,
Each moment a treasure rare.

From the hearth, light softly glows,
Binding hearts with gentle ties.
In this place where comfort grows,
Time stands still as life complies.

Flickering Fables

In the dark, a flame flickers,
Telling tales of days gone by.
Mysteries in the shadows,
As the night whispers a sigh.

Characters dance in the light,
Each story woven with care.
Imagination takes flight,
In the warmth of the air.

Legends spun from dust and dreams,
Fables born in flickering glow.
Through the night, the magic seams,
As old tales begin to flow.

Listen close to every word,
Each whisper holds a surprise.
In the flicker, wisdom stirred,
As the past forever lies.

Resilient in the Chill

Winter's breath may bite and sting,
Yet hearts remain ever bold.
In the frost, we find our spring,
Courage in the biting cold.

Branches bare, yet standing strong,
Against the tempest's fierce might.
In the silence, we belong,
Resilient through the night.

Snowflakes dance, a fleeting grace,
Nature's art lost in a swirl.
With every challenge we face,
Hope unfurls, bright as a pearl.

In the chill, our spirits rise,
Finding warmth in each small thrill.
Together, we touch the skies,
United, we are resilient still.

Flickering Dreams

In the twilight whispers, we find our way,
Stars above us, guiding the stray.
Each heartbeat echoes, a promise untold,
Flickering dreams in the night's gentle hold.

Moments of magic, caught in our gaze,
Softly they linger, through a misty haze.
Awake in the silence, but lost in the dream,
Chasing the shadows, where glimmers still beam.

Winds carry secrets, rustling the leaves,
Through the stillness, our heartache we cleave.
In this canvas of night, we paint our souls,
Flickering dreams make us powerful whole.

So let us adore these echoes and sigh,
In flickering dreams, we learn how to fly.
Together we'll dance without fear, bold and free,
While the universe whispers, just you and me.

Echoes of Shared Smiles

In a world where laughter intertwines,
Echoes of joy dance on the lines.
A single glance, a spark ignites,
Shared smiles in shadows, the heart ignites.

Moments suspended, time stands still,
In those brief instances, we find our fill.
Together we wander on this gentle road,
Carrying the warmth that shared smiles bestowed.

Whispers of kindness float in the air,
A bond unspoken, beyond mere care.
In every embrace, a story unfolds,
Echoes of laughter, our hearts, they behold.

With each gentle nod and knowing gaze,
We weave a tapestry, love's tender maze.
Forever will linger, these memories bright,
In echoes of shared smiles, we find our light.

A Dance of Light and Shadow

In the twilight glow, where contrasts play,
Light and shadow weave tales of the day.
A delicate balance, each moment a grace,
In the silent rhythm, we find our place.

Flickers of brightness touch the gloom,
As shadows lengthen, they start to bloom.
In the quiet corners, where secrets wait,
We dance with our fears, let love resonate.

Embracing the darkness, we find the spark,
A waltz of the heart, igniting the dark.
With every soft step, we learn and grow,
In the dance of light, our true selves show.

Through the tapestry woven of night and day,
We learn to cherish our own unique way.
For in this grand dance, both beauty and strife,
Light and shadow guide us through the dance of life.

Affection in the Air

In the gentle breeze, affection does sway,
Carried on whispers that love finds a way.
Through laughter and kindness, hearts come alive,
Affection in the air, where true feelings thrive.

Each glance a promise, in moments we share,
Wrapped in warmth, as we lay ourselves bare.
With every heartbeat, our souls intertwine,
In the dance of connection, hearts brightly shine.

Like petals unfolding beneath the sun's light,
Affection flourishes, banishing night.
With kindness our compass, we navigate life,
Embracing each other through joy and through strife.

So let the winds carry our love far and wide,
Affection in the air, our hearts open wide.
Together we'll wander, hand in hand, surprisingly rare,
Creating a world rich with affection in the air.

Holding the Night

Stars whisper secrets, low and bright,
Moon glows softly, holding the night.
Shadows dance gently, in twilight's fold,
Dreams take flight, as stories unfold.

The breeze carries laughter, cool and sweet,
Crickets sing softly, a rhythmic beat.
Trees sway lightly, in nature's embrace,
Time slows its march, in this sacred space.

Silhouettes breathe, beneath a sky grand,
Hearts entwined deeply, hand in hand.
With every breath, we savor the scene,
Lost in the magic, where moments convene.

In the hush of night, all fears take flight,
Wrapped in the beauty, everything feels right.
As dawn approaches, the stars take their leave,
Still holding the night, in dreams we believe.

Serenade of Shimmering Lights

Colors like whispers, paint the dark sky,
Dancing reflections, as moments pass by.
Glimmers of silver, grace every street,
A melody plays, a soft, soothing beat.

Lanterns are floating, dreams on the flow,
Illuminating hopes, in the night's gentle glow.
Voices rise softly, a chorus of cheer,
In the serenade, love draws near.

Each twinkle a promise, a wish on the breeze,
Echoes of laughter, that drift through the trees.
Every light tells a story, a tale to ignite,
Embracing the beauty, of a magical night.

As shadows give way to the dawn's embrace,
The brilliance lingers, time can't erase.
In hearts forever, this moment ignites,
The serenade lives on, in shimmering lights.

Glistening Silence

Quiet descends, a soft, gentle hush,
The world holds its breath, in the sacred crush.
Stars flicker softly, in velvet repose,
Where secrets are buried, and stillness grows.

Frost kisses ground, where whispers collide,
Nature's embrace, where mysteries hide.
Time drifts like feathers, on soft, silver streams,
In glistening silence, we find our dreams.

Shadows entwine, in the lull of the night,
Hearts beat like drummers, caught in delight.
Moments suspended, in stillness profound,
A symphony echoes, without a sound.

With dawn on the horizon, the curtain will rise,
Yet in glistening silence, the magic still lies.
A treasure of peace, in this tranquil expanse,
Where we dance with the shadows, in a timeless romance.

A Hearth's Embrace

Fires crackle softly, spreading warm light,
In the heart of the home, everything feels right.
Crisp autumn whispers, through the open door,
Inviting us closer, to gather once more.

Laughter like echoes, bounces off walls,
With stories exchanged, as the evening calls.
Blankets wrapped tightly, a snug little nest,
In this cozy corner, we find our rest.

Candles are flickering, shadows hug tight,
Every moment woven, in the warmth of night.
The scent of cinnamon, dances around,
In this hearth's embrace, true love is found.

As embers fade gently, with the dawn's first light,
Memories linger, a sweet delight.
A promise of warmth, in the days yet to trace,
Forever we cherish, a hearth's embrace.

Tea and Tranquility

Steam rises softly in the air,
A gentle brew, without a care.
Quiet sips in morning light,
Embrace the calm, hold on tight.

In china cups, stories flow,
With each sip, the worries slow.
Laughter dances, memories meet,
In this sanctuary, life feels sweet.

Herbal whispers, chamomile calm,
A fragrant touch, a soothing balm.
Moments cherished, hearts align,
In the warmth of tea, we find the divine.

As twilight falls, the kettle sings,
In the twilight, peace it brings.
With each ritual, we renew,
In tea's embrace, there's love so true.

Canvas of Night

Overhead, stars twinkle and gleam,
The night unfolds like a whispered dream.
Moonlight pools on silent streams,
Painting shadows, weaving beams.

A canvas vast, so dark, so deep,
Where secrets of the cosmos sleep.
Constellations stretch their arms wide,
Guiding sailors, the ocean's pride.

The breeze carries stories of old,
Of lovers and heroes, brave and bold.
Midnight's hush, a soft reprise,
While the heavens dance and rise.

In twilight's glow, wishes take flight,
In the quiet, hearts feel light.
Beneath the stars, we share our dreams,
Intertwined in cosmic streams.

Under Frosted Boughs

Winter whispers through the trees,
Each branch adorned with icy ease.
A world transformed by nature's hand,
Under frosted boughs, we stand.

The ground is quilted, white as snow,
In this stillness, we learn to slow.
Crunching steps on frozen trails,
Nature speaks, and the silence hails.

Sunlight glitters on crystal sheets,
A wondrous realm where magic greets.
With every breath, the cold bites slight,
Yet warmth thrives within, a gentle light.

As twilight beckons, shadows play,
With every moment, night claims day.
Under frost, hearts ignite,
In the still of winter's night.

Starlit Interludes

In the hush of dusk, dreams arise,
Beneath the vast, uncharted skies.
Glimmers shimmer in velvet black,
We journey forth, no looking back.

Whispers travel on the cool night air,
Voices echo, without a care.
Moments dance in luminous grace,
Starlit interludes, time can't erase.

The universe sings a quiet tune,
In the presence of the silver moon.
Caught in rapture, we lose track,
Of fleeting time, there's no lack.

In every star, a story told,
Of lovers lost and hearts of gold.
As night unfolds its soft embrace,
In starlit dreams, we find our place.

Coals Beneath a Blanket

The fire glows, a soft embrace,
Its warmth wraps round in tender grace.
Shadows dance on walls at night,
Whispers carry in the light.

Beneath the stars, a quiet hum,
The crackling wood, a gentle drum.
Moments shared, hearts intertwined,
In these coals, a love defined.

Outside, the chill bites at the air,
Yet here we find our refuge rare.
With every spark, a dream takes flight,
We hold on close, our spirits bright.

As dawn approaches, embers die,
Yet love remains, it doesn't lie.
With coals beneath a blanket's fold,
Our story warms, forever told.

Beneath a Silver Moon

The silver moon hangs high and bright,
Casting shadows through the night.
Whispers soft as morning dew,
In dreams, I wander close to you.

Stars like jewels in velvet skies,
Each a wish, a soft surprise.
Hand in hand, we slowly roam,
In the dark, we find our home.

The world asleep, yet we awake,
Every moment ours to take.
Beneath a sky of dreams anew,
I find my heart beating for you.

As silver beams kiss the ground,
In this stillness, love is found.
Forevermore, we'll share this tune,
A serenade beneath the moon.

Frosted Air, Warm Hearts

Winter's breath upon the trees,
Chills the air with gentle ease.
Yet within, a fire glows bright,
Filling souls with pure delight.

Frosted patterns on the glass,
Nature's art as moments pass.
In the cold, we find a spark,
Guiding us through winter's dark.

With every laugh, we warm the night,
In shared stories, hearts take flight.
Frosted air can't freeze our glee,
For love ignites, eternally.

So let the seasons turn and swirl,
Embrace the chill, the dance, the whirl.
As long as we have hearts so warm,
We'll weather any winter storm.

A Symphony of Snowflakes

In quiet falls, the snowflakes glide,
A symphony of white, they hide.
Dancing down with gentle grace,
Each a note in winter's face.

Whispers soft from sky to ground,
In their landing, joy is found.
A canvas wide, so pure, so bright,
Each flake shines in morning light.

With laughter shared, we chase and play,
In this wonderland of gray.
A frosty breath, a spark, a cheer,
The music plays when you are near.

As day turns night, the stars will gleam,
Snowflakes waltz, we start to dream.
A symphony that sings so sweet,
In every dance, our hearts will meet.